‹ EL SALVADOR ›

EL SALVADOR

Renfield Sanders

CHELSEA HOUSE PUBLISHERS
Philadelphia

Chelsea House Publishers

Contributing Author: Jeff Beneke

Copyright © 1999 by Chelsea House Publishers,
a division of Main Line Book Co.
All rights reserved.
Printed and bound in the United States of America.

3   5   7   9   8   6   4   2

Library of Congress Cataloging-in-Publication Data applied for

ISBN 0–7910–4737–7

‹CONTENTS›

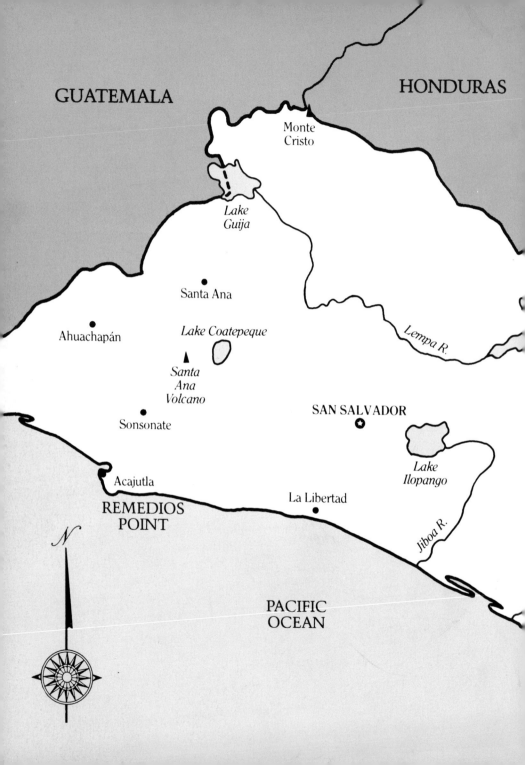

GUATEMALA

HONDURAS

Monte
Cristo

*Lake
Guija*

● Santa Ana

Lake Coatepeque

● Ahuachapán

▲
*Santa
Ana
Volcano*

Lempa R.

● Sonsonate

SAN SALVADOR
⊙

*Lake
Ilopango*

Acajutla

La Libertad
●

REMEDIOS
POINT

Jiboa R.

N

PACIFIC
OCEAN

◄ FACTS AT A GLANCE ►

Land and People

Area	8,124 square miles (21,041 square kilometers)
Highest Point	Cerro El Pital, 8,190 feet (2,730 meters)
Greatest Length	88 miles (142 kilometers)
Greatest Width	163 miles (262 km)
Major Rivers	Lempa, Torola, Grande de San Miguel
Major Lakes	Olomega, Ilopango, Coatepeque, Güija
Capital	San Salvador (population 478,000; metropolitan area, 1.5 million)
Other Major Cities	Soyapango (population 251,811); Santa Ana (population 202,337); San Miguel (population 182,817); Mejicanos (population 145,000)
Population	5,828,987
Population Density	718 people per square mile (277 per sq km)
Population Distribution	Rural, 57 percent; urban, 43 percent
Official Language	Spanish
Literacy Rate	71.5 percent (males, 73.5 percent; females, 69.8 percent)
Ethnic Groups	Mestizo, 94 percent; Indian, 5 percent; white (of European descent), 1 percent
Major Religion	Roman Catholic, 75 percent of population
Average Life Expectacy	68.9 years (males, 65.4 years; females, 72.5 years)

Economy

Major Resources	Agricultural products, hydroelectric power
Major Exports	Coffee (45 percent of export earnings), sugarcane, and cotton.
Land Use	Meadows and pastures, 29 percent; arable land, 27 percent; permanent crops, 8 percent; forest and woodland, 6 percent
Agriculture	Employs 40 percent of work force, accounts for 10 percent of total economy
Industrial Products	Food products, beverages, fertilizers, petroleum, tobacco, chemicals, textiles
Currency	Colon, divided into 100 centavos
Average Annual Income	Equal to U.S. $1,530

Government

Form of Government	Republic with one legislative house (the Legislative Assembly)
Head of State	President elected by citizens age 18 and over
Elected Officials	President, 84 members of Legislative Assembly, district and municipal councillors
Administrative Organization	14 departments, each with a governor appointed by the president, subdivided into districts and townships with elected councils and mayors
Judiciary	A ten-member Supreme Court of Justice, appointed by the Legislative Assembly, interprets the law; department and municipal courts handle civil and criminal cases

◄HISTORY AT A GLANCE►

by 3000 B.C.	The Chorotega tribes have migrated to El Salvador from central Mexico.
100 to 1000 A.D.	Western El Salvador is part of the Mayan Empire. It is occupied by a Mayan tribe called the Pokoman, who build many large limestone pyramids in the hills.
during 1000s	The warlike Pipil, related to the Aztecs of Mexico, arrive in El Salvador and take over the western part of the country from the Pokoman.
by early 1500s	The Pipil have conquered almost all of present-day El Salvador. Only a few scattered tribes have resisted their rule.
1524	Spanish *conquistadores*, under the direction of Pedro de Alvarado, arrive in El Salvador and subdue the Pipil.
1525	Alvarado founds the city of San Salvador. Three years later, it is moved to its present site because of earthquakes.
1552	The Spanish establish the city and province of Sonsonate. San Salvador and Sonsonate are governed by the captain general of Guatemala.
1786	San Salvador becomes a governorship. Around this time, many Spanish colonists in Central America begin to become impatient with Spain's administration of the colonies.
1811	José Matías Delgado and Manuel José Arce lead an unsuccessful revolt against Spanish rule in San Salvador. A similar rebellion fails in 1814.

1821	The captain general of Guatemala declares Central America independent from Spain. He tries to unite Central America with the newly formed Mexican empire. San Salvador determines not to join the Mexicans.
1823	The Mexican empire collapses. Leaders of the region form the United Provinces of Central America, including San Salvador and Sonsonate, Honduras, Guatemala, Nicaragua, and Costa Rica. Arce is voted president of the new federation.
late 1820s	Liberal and Conservative forces battle for control of the federation.
1829	Liberals in San Salvador rebel against Arce's rule.
1830	Under Francisco Morazán, a Liberal army defeats the federation. Arce resigns. Morazán becomes president.
late 1830s	Peasant uprisings and conflicts between Liberals and Conservatives tear the federation apart. By 1839, only San Salvador remains a member.
1840	Salvadoran leaders found the republic of El Salvador, including San Salvador and Sonsonate.
1840 to 1885	Liberal and Conservative forces compete for power, sometimes in bloody warfare. Heads of state and government policies change frequently and unpredictably.
after 1885	The coffee industry flourishes. The government becomes somewhat stable but continues to be controlled by a few wealthy families.
1931	El Salvador's first elected president, Arturo Araujo, is thrown out of office when General Maximiliano Hernández Martinéz seizes control of the government.
1931 to 1944	Martinéz rules as both military dictator and president. He ruthlessly suppresses all political opposition.

1944 to 1970s	A series of military takeovers and short-lived governments destroys the country's political stability. During the 1970s, the government adopts harsh measures to silence its critics.
1969	El Salvador attacks Honduras in the short but bitter Soccer War. The Organization of American States negotiates a settlement of the border dispute.
late 1970s	Opposition to the government takes the form of guerrilla and terrorist action.
1978	The army kills 30 antigovernment protesters. Archbishop Oscar Arnulfo Romero criticizes the government.
1979	A council of military officers takes control of the government and promises reform. José Napoleón Duarte is a civilian member of the council.
1980	The new government continues the repressive policies of the former regime. Archbishop Romero is assassinated, and violence between government and guerrilla forces becomes an open civil war. Duarte is appointed president.
1982	Duarte's party loses seats in the Constituent Assembly and he resigns from the presidency.
1984	Duarte is elected president.
1986	Severe earthquake kills 1,500 people.
1989	Alfredo Cristiani elected president; rebels launch major offensive against the government.
1990	United Nations sponsors peace talks between government and rebel leaders.
1992	Peace treaty signed, ending long civil war.
1994	Armando Calderón Sol elected president.

Privately cultivated home gardens have been created out of some of the former great commercial estates.

El Salvador
and the World

The republic of El Salvador (Spanish for "The Savior") lies on the Pacific coast of Central America. It borders Guatemala to the northwest, Honduras to the north and east, Nicaragua to the southeast, and the Pacific Ocean to the southwest. Ever since it was first conquered by the Spanish in 1524, El Salvador has experienced long periods of political strife. Most recently, the country was torn by a long and brutal civil war that lasted from 1979 to 1992.

During the war, much attention in the United States was focused on the 1980 murder of four American women, including three nuns. The United States was directly involved in the war, providing the government of El Salvador with millions of dollars in aid each year as well as weapons and military training. Although critical of the government's harsh policies—and especially of its human rights violations—the United States feared that the antigovernment guerrilla forces were led by Communists with ties to Cuba and the Soviet Union.

Many Americans disapproved of their government's involvement in the El Salvador conflict. They claimed that the Salvadoran government violated the civil rights of students, church leaders, and other political dissidents. Aid to El Salvador became an important political issue in the United States.

The civil war was devastating to Salvadorans. An estimated 75,000 people were killed, most of them civilians. Thousands of oth-

In the 1980s U.S. demonstrators protested U.S. support of El Salvador's regime.

ers were held in jails as political prisoners. Many Salvadorans fled the turmoil in their country. Some migrated to other Central American countries. Others, seeking refuge from political persecution at home, went to the United States and Europe.

An underlying cause of the political strife in El Salvador was the country's economy. Although El Salvador contains much extremely fertile farmland and has developed more industries than any other country in Central America, most Salvadorans are desperately poor. For centuries, a small percentage of the population has controlled a large percentage of the country's land and wealth. The Salvadorans have had difficulty changing this situation because they have not always been able to elect their leaders democratically. Often, the government has been in the hands of military juntas (councils or groups of officers that have seized control by force).

In the 1960s and 1970s, various groups of Salvadorans demanded reforms in the way the country was governed and in the laws of land ownership. The government announced some reforms, but antigovernment groups felt that they were not enough. From occasional skirmishes, the resulting conflict escalated into a full-scale civil war. The war forced El Salvador to depend on aid from other countries to feed its people and provide even limited health care. It also caused serious damage to the economy, interfering with agriculture and destroying factories, roads, buildings, and power plants. Trade and investment declined sharply.

A peace treaty was signed in January 1992, ending the 12-year-long civil war. The agreement called for both sides to lay down their guns; it also promised to reform the military and police forces and to bring about a more equitable distribution of land ownership. A commission was created to investigate the human-rights violations that occurred during the civil war. In 1993 that commission issued a report blaming the military and right-wing "death squads" for most of

the civilian deaths and human-rights violations. Some military leaders were prosecuted for their actions, but most were allowed to retire or were granted amnesty.

In March 1994, Salvadorans elected a new president, Armando Calderón Sol, and a new Legislative Assembly, which included representatives from both sides in the civil war. The country has begun the difficult process of rebuilding its economy and implementing the reforms promised in the 1992 peace treaty. But old wounds take

National Palace, shown here in 1983,
has been the site of many disturbances.

time to heal. Strong differences of opinion still divide Salvadorans, and progress has been slow in carrying out many of the promised reforms, especially those dealing with land ownership and economic democracy. Many believe that the key to long-term peace for El Salvador lies in creating a climate of political and economic freedom and opportunity for the citizens.

El Salvador's hills and valleys are rich in fertile volcanic soil and are densely cultivated.

Land of Precious Things

The Mayas, an Indian people who inhabited northern Central America before Europeans arrived in the New World, called El Salvador Cuscatlán. The name meant "The Land of Precious Things." No one today is quite sure just what things the Mayas regarded as precious. El Salvador has little gold or silver, although fertile soil abounds. Cocoa beans, which the Mayas used as money, grow well there. Perhaps chocolate was one of the "precious things" for which Cuscatlán was named.

Whatever the Maya name referred to, El Salvador is a land of great variety and potential. The country is small—8,124 square miles (21,041 square kilometers) in area. Nevertheless, it contains three mountain ranges, more than 20 volcanoes, dense tropical forests, rolling plains with pastures and farmland, several large lakes, more than 300 rivers, and an abundance of coastal harbors and beaches.

This varied topography forms the five different regions within El Salvador. From south to north, these regions are the lowlands along the Pacific coast; the southern range of low, volcanic mountains; the central plain; the valleys of the Lempa and Grande de San Miguel rivers, which cut across the central plain; and the northern mountains.

The coastal lowlands make up about 10 percent of El Salvador's area. They run along the 210 miles (338 kilometers) of the Pacific coastline. The offshore waters are deep, and no reefs or island chains protect the coast. Row after row of huge, powerful breakers pound El Salvador's beaches. The sand on these beaches startles newcomers—it is glistening black, made of powdered lava (volcanic rock), in stark contrast to the sparkling white coral sand of most tropical beaches.

Prominent features of El Salvador's coastline include Remedios Point in the west and Jiquilisco Bay in the east. Forming the southeastern border between El Salvador and Nicaragua is the Gulf of Fonseca, a large, sheltered inlet that reaches 40 miles (64 kilometers) inland and covers an area of 700 square miles (about 1,820 square kilometers). The gulf's entrance—marked by Amapula Point on the El Salvador side—is about 20 miles (32 km) across, but its widest point spans about 50 miles (81 km).

The lowlands range between 10 and 20 miles (16 and 32 kilometers) in width, with their widest point at the mouth of the Lempa River. Steep

The countryside is dotted with historical ruins, such as this one at Tazumal.

mountain spurs that run from the inland ranges to the sea without a break interrupt the lowlands. Many small, shallow streams and rivers also cut into the land along the coastline. But most of the region is covered with low, moist swamps, grasslands, or farmland. The fertile soil contains many minerals from volcanic rocks.

The source of this rich, volcanic soil is the southern mountain range. This region (just north of the coastal lowlands) accounts for 30 percent of the country's territory. The range reaches an average height of about 4,000 feet (1,200 meters) above sea level and consists of more than 20 cone-shaped volcanoes, with broad, gentle slopes between them. Like the coastal lowlands, this region is extremely fertile because of its high-quality soil.

From west to east, the southern mountain range breaks into five clusters of volcanoes. The chief peaks of the westernmost cluster are Izalco, San Marcelino, Santa Ana, Los Naranjos, Aquila, San Juan de Dios, Apaneca, Tamajaso, and La Lagunita. Next comes a smaller group containing San Salvador and Las Pavas. East of them lie San Vicente and Ciguatepeque. The next group consists of Tecapa, Taburete, Buenapa, Usulután, Chinameca, and San Miguel. Finally, Conchagua rises abruptly from the shore of the Gulf of Fonseca in the far east.

Most of these volcanoes are dead, empty cones. A few, however, are still active. Izalco, which is 6,266 feet (1,880 meters) high and lies 25 miles (40 kilometers) inland, is the liveliest. It was formed during a gigantic eruption only 150 years ago, and it continued to spit fire and smoke for decades afterward. Izalco is still called the "Lighthouse of the Pacific" because flickers of its fire and molten lava are sometimes visible from far out at sea.

Volcanic eruptions are now rare in El Salvador, but earthquakes—caused by the same geological forces that produced the volcanoes—are common. San Salvador, the country's capital, is situated about 2,200 feet (660 meters) above sea level, in a valley surrounded by volcanic peaks. Earthquakes and tremors are so common there that the area is called

Izalco is one of the largest of the many volcanoes in the southern range of mountains.

Valle de las Hamacas—the "Valley of Hammocks." According to a local saying, the ground moves more than a swinging hammock does. Earthquakes have destroyed San Salvador three times in its 450-year history.

North of the volcanic range lies a central plain that covers 25 percent of the country. With altitudes ranging between 1,300 and 2,600 feet (390 and 780 meters), the plain is a rolling plateau covered with grassy pastureland and farmland. Two deep valleys cut into it along the Lempa and Grande de San Miguel rivers. Together, these valleys make up another 20 percent of El Salvador's area. They contain a few wooded areas among terraced pastures and garden plots.

The remaining 15 percent of El Salvador comprises the northernmost region, a rugged, mountainous district along the Guatemalan and Honduran borders. Two ranges—the Metapán and the Chalatenango, named for two small villages of the region—form the backbone of the border mountains. Their height varies from 4,900 to 6,500 feet (1,470 to 1,950 meters), and their terrain contains many steep, small valleys and swiftly running mountain streams.

In the far northwestern corner of the country, where the borders of El Salvador, Guatemala, and Honduras meet, the peak Monte Cristo rises to 7,933 feet (2,380 meters). All three nations claim Monte Cristo. If it is regarded as belonging to El Salvador, it is one of that country's highest peaks.

Dozens of lakes dot the Salvadoran landscape. Many of them formed when rainwater filled the craters of extinct volcanoes. The four largest of these round, deep lakes lie in a chain across El Salvador.

The easternmost of the four is Lake Olomega. In the center of the country, 12 miles (19 kilometers) east of San Salvador, is Lake Ilopango, El Salvador's largest lake, with an area of about 25 square miles (65 square kilometers). This scenic lake, set amid lush greenery and tall peaks, is a popular resort area, surrounded by the vacation homes of the wealthy. Ilopango is something of a mystery, however. It has changed size and shape dramatically several times, for unknown reasons. In the 1880s, the lake suddenly grew much larger, bursting its bounds and flooding its shores, even though no rain had fallen. In 1928, Ilopango's waters again

Lakes such as Lake Coatepeque are formed when rainwater fills the craters of extinct volcanoes that dot the Salvadoran landscape.

swelled unexpectedly and destroyed the homes and farms on its banks. Since that time, it has remained stable and peaceful.

West of San Salvador is the nation's second largest lake, Coatepeque, with an area of 15 square miles (39 square kilometers). Far to the west, Lake Güija straddles El Salvador's border with Guatemala. Fed by rainfall and mountain streams, Güija is the source of El Salvador's major river, the Lempa.

The Lempa flows for more than 80 miles (129 kilometers) across northern El Salvador from west to east, then turns sharply south. It flows in this direction for 65 miles (105 km) through the central plateau, the southern mountain range, and the coastal lowlands before emptying into the Pacific near Jiquilisco Bay. Many smaller rivers join the Lempa as tributaries; the Torola, the chief tributary, drains the northeastern border area. Two hydroelectric power plants harness the Lempa's energy. The larger dam, in the northern part of the country, created a deep, narrow lake that winds for nearly 40 miles (64 km) through the mountain valleys.

The Grande de San Miguel, the country's second largest river, drains eastern El Salvador. Many short, turbulent streams flow down the slopes of the mountain areas, and short rivers such as the Jiboa drain areas of the coastal plain. Only the broad, southern reaches of the Lempa, however, are deep and flat enough for navigation. The other rivers of El Salvador are too steep, shallow, or choked with rapids to be navigable. Most of them flood during the rainy season and dry up during the dry season.

Climate and Weather

Although El Salvador is located in the Earth's tropical zone, its climate is truly tropical only along the coast and in the lowest regions of the Lempa River Valley. There, daytime temperatures range between 85° and 90° Fahrenheit (29° and 32° Centigrade) and nighttime temperatures seldom fall below 70° F or 75° F (21° C or 24° C). Salvadorans call these hot, low-lying areas *tierra caliente* (Spanish for "hot land").

Higher parts of the country are cooler. As a general rule, the temperature drops about 3° F (1.6° C) with each increase of 1,000 feet (300 meters) in altitude. For example, Acajutla, on the coast, has an average annual temperature of 80° F (26° C), while the average annual temperature of Santa Ana, in the interior, is 73° F (23° C); the difference in temperature is 7° F (4° C) because Santa Ana is about 2,100 ft (630 m) higher than Acajutla.

Most of El Salvador is between 2,500 and 6,000 feet (750 and 1,800 meters) above sea level. Temperatures at these altitudes are usually warm, rather than hot. Days are seldom hotter than 75° F or 80° F (24° C or 27° C); nights are comfortable, between 60° F and 70° F (15° C and 21° C). These temperatures are typical of the *tierra templada* (temperate land).

A few small areas in the higher mountains are called *tierra fría* (cold land). Daytime temperatures in the tierra fría may reach 75° F (24° C), but nights can be as cool as 50° F to 55° F (10° C to 13° C). Some nights are cold enough for frost to form.

Sticks, patched together with mud, are used to construct many peasants' huts.

El Salvador has only two seasons, *verano* and *invierno*. The difference between them is one of rainfall rather than temperature. Temperatures vary little throughout the year in El Salvador—the difference in temperature between noon and midnight is likely to be greater than that between summer and winter. *Verano* is the dry season and lasts from November through April. Harvest falls at the beginning of verano, and the season is characterized by dust, smoke, and the brown and gray colors of a dry landscape. *Invierno* is the rainy season, from May through October—the growing season for plants. Although temperatures do not change much

Warm temperatures and generous rainfall allow for long growing seasons.

from season to season, verano is generally much more comfortable because humidity is lower.

Annual rainfall in El Salvador increases with altitude. The coastal lowlands receive about 68 inches (1,727 millimeters). The drier plateau and river valleys receive between 45 and 60 inches (1,143 and 1,524 mm). But the mountain areas receive between 70 and 100 inches (1,778 and 2,540 mm). An exception is the dry region in the far northwest, north of Lake Güija. This small area at the end of the mountain ranges receives about the same amount of rain as the central plateau.

Nearly all of the country's rainfall takes place during invierno. San Salvador, for example, gets about 69 inches (1,753 millimeters) of rain each year, 63 inches (1,600 mm) of which fall between May and October. During these months, moist winds sweep inland from the Pacific Ocean. Occasionally, these moisture-laden winds precede colder, dry winds called *nortes* (from the north).

Plant and Animal Life

Trees once covered all of El Salvador. Oak and pine grew in the mountain highlands; mixed forests thrived in the slightly lower regions; thick, tropical rain forests covered a few low-lying areas; and coconut palms and mangrove swamps spread along the coast. Today, the Salvadorans have cleared much of the country for use as farmland or pastureland. They have cut or burned vast forest areas; only a small percentage of the country's original vegetation still exists.

About 6 percent of El Salvador remains forested. Impenetrable mangrove swamps (areas of short, twisted trees that grow along tropical tide lines) cover the shores of the Gulf of Fonseca. The deeper, more isolated valleys of the north still have some patches of thick woodland.

El Salvador is permitting some cleared areas to return to forest growth, for both ecological and economic reasons—timber is one of the country's most valuable resources. Among the trees found in El Salvador are cedar, laurel, and mahogany, all prized by furniture makers. The wood of the madrecacao and nispero trees is also valuable. The maquilishuat, the national tree, flourishes in the countryside and in the cities; it boasts thick foliage and vivid, scarlet blooms. Tropical fruits—melons, mangos, tamarinds, and citrus—grow widely, especially in the coastal zone.

Perhaps the most precious of El Salvador's wild plants is the tall, graceful tree called balsam of Peru. It occurs naturally only in a small area along El Salvador's Pacific coast (although it has been introduced into Sri Lanka and grows well there). The tree yields an aromatic, deep brown or black gum used to make perfume.

Balsam trees are harvested by craftsmen called *balsameros*. The balsamero climbs his tree and cuts small squares out of the trunk, then stuffs rags into the openings he has made. Next, he holds bundles of burning kindling near the holes. Heat causes the tree's sap, or balsam, to flow. The rags absorb the sap and are later boiled in huge kettles to release the balsam. Called balsam of Peru because for centuries shippers transported it to Peru before sending it on to perfumers in Europe, this fragrant sap was once believed to have medicinal properties. It is still an ingredient of folk medicines, but scientists claim that its only virtue is its exotic smell.

The vegetation of the dry area in northwest El Salvador, at the end of the mountain ranges, differs from that of the rest of the country. By cutting down the trees and allowing cattle to eat all of the grass that once grew in this area, farmers allowed the topsoil to erode. Today, poor soil and low rainfall make the area inhospitable to many plants. Mostly xerophytic plants—those that have adapted to survive on little water—such as cacti, thornbushes, and shrubs, grow there now.

Because El Salvador is so densely populated and because so much of its land has been given over to cultivation, little wildlife survives. Several centuries ago, native wildlife included jaguars, tapirs (long-snouted mammals about the size of calves), sloths (shaggy mammals that live among high tree branches), capybaras (small, piglike creatures), and armadillos. Today, only rodents, bats, reptiles, and insects are numerous on land.

Turtles and crocodiles live in almost all of the lakes and rivers, although both are now threatened with dwindling populations. The coastal waters are rich in mullet, sharks, anchovies, snappers, groupers, and grunts (so-called for the grunting noises they make when pulled out of the water).

The most varied form of wildlife in El Salvador is the bird population. Wild ducks, white herons, royal herons, bluejays, and many kinds of parrots and cockatoos live in the remaining forests. Salvadorans have hunted some species almost to extinction for their colorful feathers, which are used to make hats and jewelry. The rarest bird is the urraca. Blue and gray, with a call like a human laugh, the urraca now exists only in remote and rural areas.

A Catholic church, a common sight throughout Central America, is one of the most visible signs of the Spanish conquest.

Indians and Conquistadores

The first people known to have lived in El Salvador were American Indians. Like all native Americans, they descended from wandering Asian nomads who crossed the Bering Strait land bridge from Siberia into Alaska between 15,000 and 10,000 B.C. Within 2,000 years, these tribespeople had migrated as far south as Tierra del Fuego, at the tip of South America. Along the way, they settled in various areas throughout the Americas and developed many different cultures.

The Chorotega tribes came to El Salvador from central Mexico in about 3000 B.C. They settled in the highlands, where they lived by hunting and by raising grain and vegetables. Scholars know little about their culture except that the Chorotega were accomplished craftsmen. Archaeologists have found well-preserved pottery jars and woven baskets at the sites of old Chorotega dwellings.

To the north of the Chorotega, in what is now southern Mexico and Guatemala, a mighty civilization developed that was to flourish for centuries. The empire of the Maya Indians arose in about 500 B.C. and reached its peak of power and influence between 300 and 900 A.D. At its peak, the Maya kingdom extended into El Salvador and Honduras, where the Mayas built great cities and temples in the jungles and mountain valleys. They were a peaceful people who seldom fought their neighbors. From about

975 through 1200, the more warlike Aztec empire of central Mexico dominated the Mayas. After 1300, Mayan civilization decayed. The Mayas gradually abandoned their cities and drifted into the jungles to live in small, tribal villages.

Western El Salvador was part of the Maya civilization from about 100 to 1000 A.D. A Mayan tribe called the Pokoman came into the region, pushing the Chorotega south and east. The Pokoman built a number of huge, white, limestone pyramids in the western hills. The ruins of Pokoman temples stand today at Tazumel, west of San Salvador. These buildings are especially impressive because the Mayas possessed no metal tools and did not know how to use the wheel. Laborers probably quarried all of the temples' massive blocks with stone axes and carried them on their backs. These enormous structures most likely served as the sites of seasonal religious festivals rather than as dwellings.

The elaborate stone carvings they left behind reveal that the Mayas had sophisticated mathematical skills and a calendar more exact than those in use today; they could predict the movements of the heavenly bodies with great accuracy. Most scholars believe that Mayan society was organized around a series of religious rituals, which were based on the positions of the moon and the stars and probably intended to ensure heavy rainfall and good harvests.

The Mayas were skilled farmers. They cultivated corn, which they believed was the perfect food, given to man by the gods. They also grew melons, beans, squashes, peppers, and cacao plants, which produce cocoa beans. Hot chocolate brewed from the beans was their favorite drink, and they used the beans as money. Ancient paintings and carvings show that the Mayas, especially the men, adorned themselves with jade and shell jewelry for special occasions. They also wore brilliantly colored cloaks and headdresses woven from the feathers of tropical birds. The feathers they prized most were the crimson, green, gold, and blue tail feathers of the quetzal bird, which could be worn only by priests and noblemen. (The quetzal is now threatened with extinction in El Salvador.)

The figure in this limestone sculpture shows the prominent features typical of Mayan carving.

During the 11th century, another group of Indians arrived in El Salvador. They were an aggressive people called the Pipil. Their language, Nahuatl, was a version of the Aztec language, and the Pipil were probably related to the Aztecs. They were merchants and mercenary soldiers and may have reached El Salvador on trade or military missions sponsored by the Aztecs.

The Pipil outnumbered the Pokoman and soon seized control of western central El Salvador. They adopted the Maya name Cuscatlán for their new home, built cities, and planted crops. They also excelled at weaving, using the fiber of the *henequén* (sisal) plant as material.

By the early 16th century, the Pipil culture dominated Cuscatlán. The Pipil inhabited all of the land west of the Lempa River, except for a few isolated valleys in the far northwest where small groups of Pokoman remained. A people called the Chortis, descendants of the Chorotega, lived in the coastal lowlands east of the river. The Lenca, a small tribe whose origin is unknown, inhabited the northeast. The Pipil would probably have gone on to extend their influence eastward over the Lenca and the Chortis, but in 1524 newcomers entered El Salvador and quickly overcame the Pipil. The new arrivals were the Spanish, led by a handful of cruel, greedy, and remarkably successful men known as the *conquistadores* (conquerors).

Alvarado and After

Christopher Columbus discovered Central America at the turn of the 16th century. Within a very few years, many Spanish explorers, missionaries, and fortune hunters had followed Columbus to the New World. Then, from bases on the Caribbean islands of Hispaniola and Cuba, the Spanish began probing ever more deeply into the Central American jungle.

The forerunners of Spanish exploration and settlement in the New World were the conquistadores. They were tough, determined men who marched their small forces through the steaming jungles in heavy armor, braving disease, hunger, and wild beasts to capture Mexico, Central America, and most of South America for Spain. The conquistadores fought to win land for the Spanish crown and to win converts for the Catholic church, but most of all to win gold, silver, jewels, and estates for themselves.

Pedro de Alvarado, one of the lieutenants of Hernán Cortés, led the conquest of El Salvador. While Cortés was busy conquering the Aztecs of Mexico, he sent Alvarado and a small troop of mounted soldiers to capture Guatemala and the lands to the south. The daring, the skillful strategy, and most of all the firearms of the Spanish prevailed against a far larger number of Indians armed only with spears. The Indians were also frightened of the horsemen (they had never seen horses before) and weakened by new diseases, such as.influenza, that the invaders introduced.

Pedro de Alvarado led the conquest of El Salvador and founded the capital city of San Salvador.

After killing Tecun Uman, the Mayan prince of Guatemala, Alvarado pushed on into what is now El Salvador, reaching it in 1524. He encountered strong resistance from the warlike Pipil—one Indian bowman, in fact, pinned the conquistador to his saddle with an arrow through the thigh. Refusing to leave the field of battle, Alvarado is said to have remained in the saddle, urging his men to wipe out the Indians. Finally, the Pipil who remained alive surrendered.

The following year, Alvarado founded the city of San Salvador (meaning "Holy Savior") near an Indian town named Suchitoto. In 1528, the Spanish relocated the city 20 miles (32 kilometers) southwest to its present site, because of earthquakes. Alvarado did not remain in San Salvador; he returned to Guatemala and ruled that province with the title of captain general. By 1539, his soldiers had crushed the last trace of Indian rebellion in El Salvador.

El Salvador remained a colony of Spain for the next three centuries. In 1552, the Spanish founded the city of Sonsonate on the site of an

Indian village of the same name. From that time on, the provinces of San Salvador and Sonsonate developed independently. Each was administered by an *alcalde*, or mayor. In the smaller communities, the Spanish set up *cabildas* (councils) of white men to govern the Indians under the supervision of the alcaldes. Both provinces were part of the *audencia*, or captaincy general, of Guatemala. Spain thus regarded the two cities and their surrounding territories as part of the larger colony of Guatemala. San Salvador became an *intendencia* (governorship) in 1786; its territory included San Miguel, San Vicente, and Santa Ana.

Because they did not contain any gold or silver mines or Indian treasures, San Salvador and Sonsonate attracted fewer white settlers than did the other Central American colonies. Most of the Spanish who came to the two provinces were farmers or stock herders. Sonsonate, the smaller province, grew wealthy by exporting cocoa; San Salvador relied on cattle raising, agriculture, and the manufacture of indigo (a deep-blue dye made from the *jiquilite* plant).

In the years following the Spanish conquest, many Indians adopted the Catholic faith, the Spanish language, and some European customs—not always by choice. The Spaniards imposed a land-distribution system, called *repartimiento*. It granted to wealthy or powerful Spanish subjects not only huge tracts of land, but also the local inhabitants. Under this system, many Indians were forced to work as peons (peasants who owned no land) on these estates.

This rural homestead has a main house of stucco construction and storage shed built of sticks.

The Indian way of life also suffered from the Catholic church's practice of *reducción*, which involved moving the natives out of their scattered villages and into compact, centralized settlements at the Spanish missions. According to the church, reducción was intended to ease the task of educating and converting the Indians, but the practice also made it easier for the Spanish to control the Indians and prevent rebellions.

During the late 18th century, Spain's colonies in the New World became impatient with Spanish rule. All government and administration came from Madrid, and the colonists had little or no influence at the Spanish court. The native-born Latin Americans, called Creoles, resented the high taxes the Spanish government forced them to pay, and they resented the government's rule forbidding the colonies to sell their products to any country other than Spain.

It appeared that Spain had only one plan for its colonies: to drain them dry, without regard for their future. Many business and church leaders began to complain that the colonies should have a greater say in their own government. Observing the American and French revolutions then taking place, some Latin Americans went even further: they spoke of revolution and independence. After the turn of the 19th century, San Salvador became the center of revolutionary activity in Central America.

A casualty of El Salvador's civil war, the "Golden Bridge" was destroyed in an early-morning guerrilla attack.

Independence
and War

Central America's first act of defiance toward Spanish rule took place in San Salvador in 1811. Hoping to help San Salvador achieve independence, a Salvadoran priest named José Matías Delgado led a revolutionary movement, aided by his nephew, Manuel José Arce. Their actions were inspired by those of a Mexican priest named Miguel Hildalgo, who was active in Mexico's fight for independence from Spain.

Delgado's attempted revolt failed. He tried again—and failed again—in 1814. But his actions caused people throughout Central America to think and talk even more about the possibility of independence.

When the Central American colonies finally achieved independence from Spain, they did so almost by accident. On the morning of September 15, 1821, the last captain general of Guatemala (which still included all of Central America except Panama) met with his advisors in the government palace in Guatemala City. A rumor soon flew around the city that independence was being discussed at the palace. Crowds gathered in the plaza outside the palace windows. People cheered, sang, and roared their approval. Church bells rang out. Everyone believed that the captain general was about to declare independence.

And so he did. Influenced by his counselors—and perhaps by the roar of the eager crowds outside his windows—the captain general wrote out a

Manuel José Arce was elected in 1825 as first president of the United Provinces of Central America.

declaration, signed it, and read it to the public. Central America, from the Mexican border through Costa Rica, was now independent. Spain was too distracted with political trouble at home and in Mexico to try to recapture its former colonies.

The former captain general, unwilling to turn his power over to an elected congress, attempted to join the Central American provinces to the newly formed Mexican empire of General Augustín de Iturbide. San Salvador, however, refused to become part of Mexico, and the Salvadorans, led by Delgado and Arce, declared their independence from Guatemala. Iturbide sent an army under General Vicente Filisola to subdue them, and although they resisted for several months, they finally succumbed in 1822.

In 1823, Iturbide's short-lived Mexican empire collapsed, to the joy of the Salvadorans. Filisola, unable or unwilling to return to Mexico, asked the leaders of the Central American provinces to meet in Guatemala City to plan a new government. Although he hoped that the provinces would ask him to be their ruler, he was disappointed. The leaders met, agreed to form a federation, and ordered the general to depart.

The assembly of leaders, mostly upper-class Creoles, declared themselves a completely independent republic, the United Provinces of Central America. Guatemala, Nicaragua, Honduras, Costa Rica, and San Salvador (including Sonsonate) were the member states. They drew up a constitution that called for a federal capital and president in Guatemala City, and a president in each of the five states; it also abolished slavery but limited voting to landowning members of the upper class. In elections held in 1825, these voters elected Manuel José Arce president of the federation.

Arce began as a member of the Liberal party, which supported progress, change, and a redistribution of wealth and power. The opposing Conservatives favored tradition and wanted wealth and power to remain in the hands of the church and a few old families. Conflict between the Liberals and Conservatives began when Arce was elected and continued to trouble the federation for many years.

Soon after his election, Arce began to disagree with his party. He joined the Conservatives and tried to rule as a dictator. In response, the Liberals of San Salvador led a rebellion against the federation. Arce's troops besieged the city in late 1829. Thus began a period of political seesawing from Liberal to Conservative control and back again.

In 1830, a Liberal Honduran army led by Francisco Morazán defeated the federal forces. Morazán arrived in San Salvador as a victorious liberator, then marched on Guatemala City. Arce resigned his office. He and other leading Conservatives were forced to leave the federation, and Morazán was elected its president.

Arce tried twice to invade and reclaim Central America, once from Mexico and once from Cuba. His efforts were unsuccessful. But Morazán's presidency faced other problems: economic and social unrest in San Salvador, a Conservative uprising in Honduras, and opposition from the church. In 1834, Morazán moved the federation's capital to San Salvador in an attempt to weaken Conservative influence. But in 1837, the Conservatives managed to make the uneducated peasants and Indians believe that the Liberal government was responsible for an epidemic of the deadly disease cholera. Encouraged by the Conservatives, the peasants and Indians revolted against the federation. A charismatic mestizo (a person of mixed European and Indian descent) named Rafael Carrera led the revolt and overthrew the state government of Guatemala.

The revolt was the beginning of the end for the United Provinces of Central America. By April 1839, all the states except San Salvador had withdrawn from the federation. Still a Liberal stronghold, San Salvador clung to the hope of reuniting the federation. But Carrera sent Conservative forces into San Salvador from Guatemala, drove the Liberals into exile, and inflicted a disastrous defeat on the remnants of Morazán's Liberal army in 1840.

That same year, San Salvador's leaders announced the formation of the republic of El Salvador, combining the provinces of San Salvador and Sonsonate. Carrera appointed his friend Francisco Malespin the first president of El Salvador, but in 1845 the Liberals regained control after a bloody civil war. The Conservatives, however, ruled again from 1852 to 1860.

El Salvador's best-known Liberal president, General Gerardo Barrios, governed from 1860 to 1863. He founded the nation's first university and its merchant marine service. He also incorporated freedom of religion into the law and promoted agricultural and industrial projects that helped modernize the country. In recognition of his importance to his nation's development, El Salvador has officially named Barrios a national hero.

After Barrios' short, progressive presidency, El Salvador alternated between Liberal and Conservative rule throughout the rest of the 19th century. Guatemala tried twice to restore the old federation. In the second attempt, Guatemalan president Justo Rufino Barrios led his so-called federal army into El Salvador. The Salvadorans killed Barrios at the Battle of

Chalchuapa on April 2, 1885, and the United Provinces of Central America was finally and completely laid to rest.

After 1885, conflicts between Liberals and Conservatives became less violent and El Salvador gained some political stability. But power remained in the hands of a wealthy few because each president chose his successor. From 1913 to 1927, in fact, the office repeatedly passed back and forth among two brothers, Carlos and Jorge Meléndez, and a friend, Alfonso Quiñónez Molina.

One of the most important influences in El Salvador after 1885 was the growth of the coffee industry. Coffee had been introduced to the country in 1840; according to local legend, it was brought in by a Brazilian schoolteacher who missed his morning cup and planted a few coffee beans in his garden. Whether this story is true or not, coffee quickly surpassed cocoa, indigo, timber, and fruit to become El Salvador's major export product. Coffee plantations provided work for a growing number of peons, British and American companies built railroads to bring the coffee out of El Salvador's interior, and the port at La Unión bustled with activity.

Since the mid-1800s, coffee has been a leading crop in El Salvador.

Modern History

El Salvador's history entered a new phase when Pío Romero Bosque, president from 1927 to 1931, decided *not* to choose his successor. He wanted to give the Salvadorans a chance to elect their next leader. Unfortunately, Bosque's democratic intentions failed. Many candidates ran for office, but none of them won a majority of the votes. The legislature named Arturo Araujo, one of the candidates, president. After only a few weeks in office, however, Araujo was deposed when his vice president, General Maximiliano Hernández Martinéz, seized power with the help of the army.

Martinéz ruled as a military dictator and ruthlessly suppressed all opposition. The year after he took power was the bloodiest Latin America had yet seen—his soldiers killed more than 30,000 people (4 percent of the country's population) who objected to his tyrannical rule. Despite such violence, he was elected president in 1935 and 1939. Martinéz showed little regard for human rights or for the welfare of the poor, but he did make some important improvements in El Salvador's material prosperity: he started a new coinage system, founded a national bank, completed the Inter-American Highway across the country, and continued to develop the coffee export business (which was controlled by the state). But when he tried to extend his term of office in 1944, a revolution led by students and a small democratic segment of the army forced him to resign.

During the next 25 years, El Salvador saw a rapid succession of elections and coups (military takeovers of government). Most of the country's leaders were army officers who seized power, then set out to silence critics of their rule. Their harsh regimes created unrest, which eventually grew into a vicious circle of suppression and revolt. Each new leader, in turn, was overthrown—sometimes after only days—by another. In the meantime, wealthy landowners profited from the sale of coffee and cotton, but the standard of living for the poor inhabitants of both the countryside and the cities remained very low.

This period also saw the formation of many new political parties in El

Salvador, as student and worker groups began to demand a share of political power. The most powerful new parties were the Partido Revolucionario de Unificación Democratica (PRUD), which controlled the country from 1950 to 1960; the Partido de Conciliación Nacional (PCN), which replaced PRUD as the leading power during the 1960s; the Partido Demócrata Cristiano (PDC), which represented students, workers, and liberals and usually opposed government policy; and the Partido Acción Renovadora (PAR), which had Communist leanings. Some of these parties remain important to Salvadoran politics today.

The Soccer War

Beginning in the late 1950s, many poor and unemployed country dwellers migrated from crowded El Salvador across the border into Honduras, where they settled on unoccupied land. By 1969, as many as 300,000 Salvadorans were living illegally in Honduras. At that point, the Honduran government began to fear that El Salvador intended to claim some Honduran territory along the border, and it ordered the immigrants out. It imprisoned several thousand before allowing them to return to El Salvador. This incident kicked off a short but bitter war between El Salvador and Honduras. It was called the Soccer War because it took place immediately after a three-game international soccer series that greatly increased the hostility between the two countries.

In the 1980s, President José Napoléon Duarte struggled to balance the demands of right-wing elements and left-wing insurgents.

El Salvador bombed Honduran airports and sent troops across the border on July 14, 1969. The Hondurans retaliated with bombing raids of their own. By July 29, however, the Organization of American States (OAS) had negotiated a settlement, and Salvadoran troops withdrew from Honduras.

Over the next 11 years, the two nations attempted to reach an agreement. The border remained in dispute until 1980, when they finally signed a peace treaty. In the meantime, El Salvador suffered from the loss of trade with Honduras, Nicaragua, and Costa Rica (allies in the border dispute). El Salvador's economy was further strained when the 300,000 jobless, homeless, and impoverished immigrants returned from Honduras.

Civil War

Economic troubles and a growing desire for more political freedom caused widespread unrest among El Salvador's peasant class during the 1970s. Many university students joined the workers in strikes and protests; some Catholic clergymen also spoke out against the government.

In 1972, the PCN candidate, Colonel Arturo Armando Molina, won the presidential election. But his opponents claimed that if the ballots had been fairly counted, the PDC candidate, José Napoleón Duarte, would have won. Duarte supported an attempt to overthrow the Molina government; the coup failed and Duarte was exiled.

The PCN won again in 1977, when General Carlos Humberto Romero was elected. The PDC claimed that this election, too, had been rigged and the PDC candidates had been forcibly prevented from running. In the meantime, the old PAR was reorganized into the Movimiento Nacional Revolucionario (MNR), a Communist-inspired group that sometimes cooperated with the PDC in protests against the government. By the late 1970s, those protests had given way to guerrilla and terrorist acts, such as bombings, kidnappings, and assassinations. The Molina and Romero regimes retaliated by forming government terrorist squads that killed critics of the government.

(continued on p. 57)

SCENES OF
EL SALVADOR

⋏ *At dawn, lights set off the city of San Salvador against the backdrop of the surrounding mountains.*

⋎ *Most Salvadoran villages, like this one, are set amid forests, hillsides, rivers, and lakes in a lush landscape.*

▲ Volcanic peaks, largely inactive, tower over fertile countryside that is shaken periodically by earthquakes.

▼ Near San Salvador is Los Chorros park, where visitors may view examples of El Salvador's great variety of plants and vegetation.

➤ *A typical Salvadoran handicraft is the weaving of straw hats.*

∨ *Artisans throughout the land are adept at the ancient craft of pottery.*

◄ Colorful piñatas like this one are favorites at parties and festivities.

∨ Craftsmen in small factories and shops construct sturdy and practical wicker furniture and accessories.

◄ *Corn is a favorite crop in local gardens.*

➤ *Small rural homesteads are almost always handbuilt and often have tin roofs.*

❯ *Some of El Salvador's beaches are unique for their black sand. It is powdered volcanic rock.*

➤ *Like children everywhere, these young Salvadorans find time to play in seemingly inhospitable surroundings.*

∨ *Peasants buy, sell, and trade their wares and produce at open-air markets.*

(continued from p. 48)

In 1978, the army killed 30 protestors who were demanding land and financial aid for the poor. After this massacre, El Salvador's archbishop, Oscar Arnulfo Romero, became the government's harshest critic. From the cathedral in San Salvador, he claimed that the protest movement would continue as long as the government used violence against its people.

In January 1979, the Inter-American Commission on Human Rights announced that General Romero's regime was torturing and murdering political prisoners. Violence from both government and antigovernment forces continued to grow. In October, a military junta took over from Romero and promised reforms in the areas of human rights and economic benefits. Duarte returned from exile as a civilian member of the junta.

The new government began to carry out some of its promised reforms. It took over many large farms belonging to wealthy Salvadorans, giving some of the farmland to peasants and keeping the rest as government property. But the opposition movement was not satisfied with these small measures. In addition, the police and army continued their terrorist activities. Public violence exploded when Archbishop Romero was shot and killed at the altar of the cathedral in March 1980; government opponents claimed that the army had assassinated him. The situation worsened when soldiers at the national palace fired on angry mourners at Romero's funeral. The funeral became a massacre and El Salvador plunged into open civil war.

By the end of the year, the death toll on both sides had reached 22,000. On December 3, 1980, soldiers shot four American women who were sympathetic to the guerrilla movement; three of them were nuns. That same month, guerrilla and antigovernment groups joined to form the Frente Demócrata Revolucionario (FDR) and pledged to bring democracy and social reform to El Salvador. In an attempt to end the war, the junta appointed the popular Duarte president on December 13. He declared that his regime would write a new constitution and that the country would hold elections in 1982.

During 1981, violence in El Salvador continued. More than 13,000 people lost their lives. The United States, fearing that Communist elements in the FDR would gain control of the country, provided the Duarte government with money, arms, and military advisors. The government, however, was unable to subdue the guerrillas, who preferred economic destruction to open combat. By mid-1982, they had attacked 45 bridges, 20 railway lines, and more than 650 electrical generators in rural areas.

El Salvador held elections for the Constituent Assembly, its legislative body, in March 1982. The FDR did not participate in the elections, but candidates from five parties won seats. The most powerful of these

Voting stations, such as this one in San Salvador, help Salvadorans participate in the election process and further the peaceful transition of government.

parties were the PDC, the PCN, and the Alianza Republicana Nacionalista (called Arena), a very conservative, progovernment group. Major Roberto d'Aubuisson, the leader of Arena, was elected president of the assembly. Because his PDC party had not won a majority of the seats in the assembly, Duarte resigned from the presidency. He was replaced by a "temporary president," banker Alvaro Magana Borjo, who governed until the May 1984 elections.

In 1984, Duarte defeated d'Aubuisson to become president. Immediately after the election, Salvadoran courts tried and convicted the national guardsmen accused of murdering the American women; the officer accused of ordering the killings was freed on a legal technicality. The government ordered several other officers believed to have been involved in terrorist activity and assassinations expelled from the army or assigned to diplomatic posts in other countries.

Following Duarte's election, several meetings took place between the government and rebels, but no agreements could be reached to stop the fighting. In the 1989 elections, which the rebels boycotted, Arena won a majority in the Legislative Assembly, and its new leader, Alfredo Cristiani, became president. The guerrillas then launched a major offensive, which forced the government to participate in new peace talks.

In 1990, peace talks finally began under the supervision of the United Nations. In September of the following year, Cristiani and the rebel leaders agreed on the details of a peace settlement, which was formalized in a treaty in January 1992. In the 1994 elections, Armando Calderón Sol of Arena easily defeated former guerrilla leader Rubén Zamora to become the new president of El Salvador.

Mestizos, the largest ethnic group of the Salvadoran population, combine the physical characteristics of European and Indian stocks.

The Salvadorans

El Salvador has fewer ethnic groups (people of different racial and national origins) than do most Latin American countries. Nearly 94 percent of the country's 5,828,987 inhabitants are mestizo (of mixed European and Indian ancestry), descended from the children of Spanish colonists and Indian women. About 5 percent of the population is Indian. The remaining 1 percent is white.

The mestizo population combines the physical characteristics of Europeans and Indians in varying degrees. Some Salvadorans have the short, stocky build, dark, reddish-brown skin, straight, thick, black hair, and narrow eyes of the Indians; others are taller with lighter skin and hair, although fair coloring is quite rare. The small population of whites who have never intermarried with the Indians includes a few people from the Middle East; they are called *arabes* or *turcos*.

The Indians are mostly descendants of the Pipil and are concentrated in the southwestern part of the country. Some of them live in the Izalco region, but a group called the Pancho Indians lives in the village of Panchimalco, near San Salvador. A few small Lenca villages survive in the east.

All three groups—mestizo, white, and Indian—speak Spanish, the official language of El Salvador. When the Spanish arrived in the region, the chief Indian languages were Nahuatl in the west and Poton in the east. Today, Poton has died out. Nahuatl is still spoken by some Indians, but its use declines each year. The government and the University of El Salvador have started a special school to record and preserve Nahuatl.

Social and Economic Status

Social classes in El Salvador are based primarily on economic status. As in most Latin American countries, the social structure consists of a very

The great majority of Salvadorans show their Indian descent in their almond-shaped eyes and dark hair.

small, wealthy upper class and a very large, poor lower class. El Salvador's upper class is called *la primera* or *la sociedad*, or sometimes *los catorces* ("the fourteen"), because it originally consisted of 14 important families. The lower class—workers, peasants, and the unemployed—is called *la segunda* or *los pobres*. Social relationships or marriages between the two classes are extremely rare. A third group, a middle class of educated professional and business people, began to appear during the 1970s and 1980s. As yet, this middle class is quite small. If its numbers increase, however, El Salvador's middle class could become an important new element in politics and culture.

In addition to its ethnic and economic categories, Salvadoran society is further divided into two cultural categories: the *ladinos* and the Indians. A ladino is anyone—rich or poor, white, mestizo, or Indian—who wears Western-style clothes and follows Spanish-American customs. All whites and mestizos are ladinos. And some Salvadorans who are ethnically Indians, but who have abandoned the traditional Indian way of life for that of the Spanish, are considered to be ladinos like their mestizo neighbors.

Some 75 percent of Salvadorans are Roman Catholic. The number of Protestants grew significantly in the 1980s and 1990s.

Religion

Religion is an important part of El Salvador's Spanish heritage. More than 75 percent of the population is Roman Catholic. The percentage of Catholics was even higher until evangelical Protestant groups became active in the 1980s and 1990s. Some country people, especially Indians, have blended the Catholic faith with traces of the old Indian faiths. They attend the Catholic mass, for example, but bring baskets of corn to church to be blessed by the priest, just as their Mayan ancestors offered corn and other gifts to their gods. They sometimes pray to the ancient gods of wind, rain, and fertility, as well as to the Christian saints.

Religious customs form part of almost every Salvadoran's life. Some rural areas do not have churches, and traveling priests visit them only

three or four times each year. In such villages, the priest's arrival signals a flurry of baptisms, confirmations, marriages, and funeral services. Most villages, however, have churches, as do all towns and cities.

Among the religious customs most widely practiced in El Salvador are prayers said at home to the patron saint of each house and the novena (nine nights of prayer) said after a death. Easter and Christmas are national religious celebrations, and Salvadoran families usually spend these holidays together. During the civil war, government and guerrilla forces often agreed to a short cease-fire at Christmastime, so that the highways could remain open and people could visit their relatives in safety.

From July 24 to August 6 each year, Salvadorans celebrate the feast of the Holy Savior of the World with folk dancing, parades, and fireworks.

A priest blesses pipes and other materials installed by World Health Organization engineers to bring a town a steady flow of fresh, drinkable water.

The biggest religious occasion each year, however, is the *fiesta*, or feast, of the patron saint of each town or village. These saint's day fiestas often last as long as a week and include singing and dancing, lotteries, carnivals, flea markets, and dozens of parties. In some communities, societies called *cofradía*, or religious brotherhoods, organize and pay for the fiestas, with the help of the townspeople, who contribute money or labor.

One other feature of Salvadoran religious life affects almost everyone. It is the *compadrazgo*, or the relationship between the father of a child and his *compadre*, the child's godfather. The godfather does not merely appear at the child's baptism and marriage; he plays an important role in the family's life, contributing advice and even money to help the father raise the child. It is considered a great honor to be asked to be a compadre, and two men in a compadrazgo are regarded as something like blood brothers.

Although El Salvador is a crowded country, its population is distributed unevenly. About 60 percent of the population lives in the coastal and southern volcanic regions. These two regions also contain nearly all of the cities with 10,000 or more inhabitants.

Another 25 percent of the population lives in the central plain region and the river valleys, mainly in small towns and rural farming communities. The remaining 15 percent lives in the northern mountains, a region that has no towns or cities. Outside of a few villages, people live on scattered farms in the deep, widely separated valleys. Some communities in this part of El Salvador are almost entirely cut off from the outside world by their remoteness, inaccessibility, and poverty.

Family Life and Customs

The Salvadoran family has traditionally been the basic unit of Spanish-American culture. According to custom, families—usually including grandparents, aunts, uncles, and cousins—tended to be large and to live together under one roof. Married children who set up their own households usually did so in the same village or neighborhood as their parents.

Within the family, the oldest man made all the decisions and controlled the finances. His wife and children were expected to obey him without question, and respect for the family honor was a much-prized virtue.

Today, conditions in El Salvador have changed some aspects of this traditional way of life. Young men are more likely to leave home, either to join the army or to work in a different city. Young women, too, are beginning to attend school more often and to look for jobs outside their homes. Many men are forced to move around the country looking for work, leav-

A marketplace in San Salvador offers a colorful selection of local fruits and vegetables.

ing their families behind. Common-law marriage (without a church cere-mony or a license) occurs more and more frequently. As a result of these disruptions to the traditional family, El Salvador's orphanages have grown crowded, and their funding has been poor. Thousands of children work as street vendors, many of them homeless and living on the streets of San Salvador.

Wealthy and middle-class urban Salvadorans dress Western-style: dresses for the women and suits for the men. Women rarely wear pants, but jeans are popular among young men. The poorer ladino men and the Indian men wear a year-round outfit of white cotton shirt and trousers and leather sandals or sneakers. Country men always wear hats, usually large hats woven of palm leaves, with floppy brims to shade their faces and necks from the sun. Country women wear ankle-length skirts and loose blouses, most often in dark colors. They almost always wear shawls or scarves, with which they cover their heads if a stranger approaches. Most Salvadorans have only two or three sets of clothes and save the best for church.

The basic national diet consists of corn (baked into flat, round loaves of bread) and beans; onions, chili peppers, and other spices are used to add flavor to the fried beans. Most people also eat fruit at least once a day. Meat and cheese make up only 12 percent of the typical Salvadoran's food. The wealthier Salvadorans, however, eat much more beef, which is a symbol of high social status.

All Salvadorans, even children, breakfast on coffee and bread. They eat their largest meal in the middle of the day, and often follow it with a *siesta*, or short nap. In the late afternoon or evening, those who can afford it have a snack or light meal. Sometimes this consists of a *papusa*, a Salvadoran specialty consisting of a cornmeal cake stuffed with chopped meat and spices, which is sold in outdoor stalls. As in the days of the Mayas, hot chocolate is a favorite drink. The Salvadorans also consume huge quantities of candy and soft drinks made from the cocoa and sugar-cane produced in their country.

This Indian rug has motifs woven in straw.

Arts and Handicrafts

El Salvador's chief handicrafts are weaving and basket-making. Men and women alike practice these crafts in the country villages and carry their wares into the towns or cities for sale in the weekly outdoor markets. Every August, craftspeople from all over the country bring their goods to a special crafts fair in San Salvador. Some villages or regions specialize in certain crafts. For example, the village of Sesuntepeque, where a number of the surviving Lenca Indians live, is noted for its palm-leaf hats. Other communities produce rope, *petates* (sleeping mats of woven straw), saddle-bags, and hammocks made from henequen, reeds, and other sturdy fibers.

Sophisticated, urban Salvadorans tend to admire North American and European styles of music and dance. In the rural areas, though, folk music and dancing are still practiced, and folk dance troupes often entertain city-dwellers at fiestas. Two noted folk dances, versions of Mayan rain dances, are the dance of the mountain pig and the *jeu jeu*. Jeu jeu dancers in the Izalco region dress as savages and act out a mock battle between the Indians and the Spanish.

Music pervades Salvadoran culture. Musicians use the guitar, the *chirimia* (a kind of flute), and the drum. The most popular instrument, however, is the *marimba*, a piano-like instrument with keys made of hollow gourds. As many as nine people can harmonize on the marimba keyboard, striking the gourds with padded sticks to produce delicate chimes. Marimba bands enliven every fiesta and wedding, and each year a marimba festival is held in San Miguel. Bands from all over the country set up their marimbas on the street corners, and people dance in the streets day and night for a week. Some composers, such as Maria de Baratta, have used the instruments and rhythms of rural folk music in orchestral compositions, now performed all over the world.

El Salvador has produced several distinguished writers. The best known are the poet Francisco Antonio Gavidia, the philosopher Alberto Masferrer, and the historian Jorge Larde. Poetry has long been the most popular form of literature, but some young Salvadoran writers are now producing novels, often with political or revolutionary themes.

The country has four daily newspapers, with a total circulation of about 290,000, all published in San Salvador. Weekly provincial newspapers are put out in other cities. There are also ten television stations and about 100 licensed radio stations. The constitution guarantees freedom of the press, and in recent years journalists have been able to criticize the government without facing censorship or persecution.

In large towns, indoor markets offer the chance to purchase an enormous variety of fresh and prepared foods.

Town and Country

About 57 percent of Salvadorans live in rural areas, on farms or in small villages. The other 43 percent live in cities and towns, mostly in the southern region.

San Salvador is El Salvador's largest city, as well as its capital. Its population is 478,000. Earthquakes destroyed it in 1854, 1873, and 1917, and it was flooded in 1934, but the Salvadorans rebuilt it each time. Today, San Salvador is a modern city, with skyscrapers, sleek office buildings, wide streets, and large parks and plazas. Because it has been reconstructed so many times, it no longer contains any homes or churches from the colonial period.

In addition to being the center of government, San Salvador is the country's commercial center. Factories on its outskirts produce processed food, beverages, textiles, leather goods, pharmaceuticals, wood products, and cigarettes. San Salvador also contains the national cathedral, the National Museum of Science and Industry (founded in 1883), and the National Museum of El Salvador (founded in 1940 and filled with Mayan relics). The University of El Salvador was established in the capital in 1841, the much smaller Central American University in 1965.

San Salvador's suburbs have grown greatly since the early 1970s. The largest are Soyapango, with a population of 251,811; Mejicanos, with a population of 145,000; and Ciudad Delgado, with a population of 104,790.

Santa Ana is the largest city in El Salvador outside of the San Salvador metropolitan area. It was an Indian town before the Spanish arrived. It has been called Santa Ana since 1708 and is the commercial and cultural center of the western part of the country. Its population is 202,337.

Situated 10 miles (16 kilometers) northeast of Santa Ana volcano, the city lies in the heart of the country's coffee-producing district. It is the

major coffee-processing center and contains the world's largest coffee mill, the El Molino mill. Other industries include liquor distilling and the manufacture of furniture and textiles. Energy for homes and factories comes from a hydroelectric dam across the Lempa River, at its outlet from Lake Güija.

Santa Ana has a beautiful old church, El Calvario, built by the Spanish during the colonial era; it also has a more modern cathedral. A branch of the University of El Salvador is located there, and archaeological studies

San Salvador, nestled in surrounding hills, has a few low-rise buildings and some light industry.

are under way at the ruined Indian city of Chalchuapa, located 9 miles (14 kilometers) to the west.

San Miguel is the largest city in eastern El Salvador. It was founded by the Spanish in 1530, on the west bank of the Grande de San Miguel River at the foot of two volcanoes, San Miguel and Chinameca. Almost leveled by the great earthquake of 1917, San Miguel was quickly rebuilt and now has 182,817 inhabitants.

Located near the country's two biggest highways and a railway junction, San Miguel is an important center of business and trade. Its factories produce textiles, rope, and leather goods; its markets sell sugarcane, coffee, cotton, and grain from nearby fields.

San Miguel's oldest surviving building is an 18th-century cathedral. The city also has a small branch of the University of El Salvador. Like other Salvadoran cities, San Miguel suffered disruption and some damages in the civil war between 1979 and 1992.

Ahuachapán, in the far west near La Lagunita volcano and the small Molino River, has a population of 63,500. It was a Pipil town called Gueciapam when the Spanish arrived, and it received its current name in 1823. Its chief industry is coffee processing. Hot mineral springs near Malacatiupan Falls, outside the city, have formed natural baths that many Salvadorans believe can cure arthritis and other diseases. The springs are also a source of energy; a power plant that converts their heat to electricity began operating in 1975.

Sonsonate, southeast of Ahuachapán, was founded in 1552, and today its population has reached almost 61,000 people. A road and a railway connect Sonsonate with the port city of Acajutla, 12 miles (19 kilometers) away. During the colonial period, Sonsonate and Acajutla prospered in the cocoa trade. Today, their chief exports are coffee, sugarcane, fruit, and hides. Sonsonate has three noteworthy religious monuments: the colonial church of El Pilar, a small cathedral ornamented with 17 elaborately carved cupolas, and the church of Antonio del Monte. Each year, thousands of Salvadorans make pilgrimages to Antonio del Monte, hoping to be cured of illness or blindness.

Acajutla, with a population of 36,000, is El Salvador's largest and busiest seaport. It also has an oil refinery, a fertilizer plant, and a fish-processing industry. Developers have established beach resorts near Acajutla, but they have not been very successful—perhaps because the local industries make the environment somewhat unattractive.

Acajutla, El Salvador's largest and most modern port, ships the bulk of the nation's coffee exports.

La Unión, at the base of Conchagua Volcano on the Gulf of Fonseca in the east, has a population of 43,000. Its chief industry is the manufacture of jewelry and trinkets from tortoiseshell. The nearby port of Cutuco is the country's second largest seaport. The area around La Unión is noted for cattle and poultry raising, and the port handles much shipping of livestock products.

On the seacoast south of San Salvador lies La Libertad, a quiet town of 22,800. In colonial days, La Libertad was a bustling port, the chief center for the shipping of balsam. In 1976, it was closed to international shipping. Today, it has a small fishing industry and a few beach hotels and resorts. Palm trees, houses painted with fading whitewash, and old, wrought-iron balconies give La Libertad the look of 19th-century Latin America.

Throughout the country, the upper class lives in spacious villas, or mansions, on large estates. These estates are usually walled and protected by private armed guards. Middle-class families generally live in small row houses or large urban apartments. The poorer masses, in contrast, live in crowded, one-room apartments in the cities; most cities have growing slum areas where the poorest people live, sometimes in shacks made of cardboard or scrap lumber.

In the country, many farmers live in small, square houses (only one story high to prevent damage from earthquakes) made of sun-baked adobe brick, with dirt floors and roofs of thatched straw. Extremely poor peasants live in huts made of woven sticks plastered together with mud. Roads and streets remain largely unpaved.

Wealthy Salvadorans generally furnish their homes in sophisticated European style. The furniture of the rural ladino or the Indian, however, is simpler: a chair or two, a wooden table, perhaps an old bureau or cupboard, and a petate. Indoor plumbing is unknown outside the cities and the estates of the big landowners. If they are lucky, the peasants get water for drinking, cooking, and washing from a village tap; if not, they dig their own wells or carry water from a stream.

El Salvador's cities and towns are growing fast. Most land suitable for agriculture is already occupied, so young people drift into the cities looking for work. But urban businesses and industries cannot provide jobs for all the unemployed, particularly as many of them have little or no education. It is likely that El Salvador's urban unemployed population will continue to grow—and crime, social unrest, and disease may increase along with it.

A Peace Corps volunteer teaches youngsters vegetable gardening techniques to improve the yield of family plots.

Economy and Transportation

El Salvador's most important resource is its fertile volcanic soil, which allows farming and herding throughout much of the country. A total of 70 percent of the country is covered with farmland (35 percent), pastures (29 percent), and forest (6 percent). Of the farmland, only about 15 percent requires artificial irrigation.

Mineral resources are sparse. The country has a few small deposits of gold, silver, and sulfur, but most are too remote to be mined economically. Gold and silver are mined in limited quantities near San Sebastian, in the central region. El Salvador has no coal or oil; the Salvadorans import oil for their energy needs from Venezuela. Since the 1970s, however, hydro-electric and geothermal power plants have contributed a significant percentage of the country's energy—although guerrilla attacks on power plants and generators created setbacks in the energy program.

For hundreds of years before the Spanish arrived, the Indians gathered salt from a few shallow lagoons and tidepools on the Pacific coast. Salt was a highly prized trade commodity in the Indian and colonial years, and it is still mined in a few places in coastal El Salvador. The coastal area also has a small fishing industry that catches about 11,760 tons (13,000 metric tons) of seafood—mostly shrimp—each year. Most of the shrimp is sold to the United States.

For centuries, agriculture dominated El Salvador's economy. Today, farming and herding together make up only about one-tenth of the country's economy, although they occupy two-fifths of the work force. Two kinds of farming are practiced: subsistence farming and cash-cropping.

Families who practice subsistence farming produce enough food to support themselves, with little left over for sale. Most subsistence farmers own or rent small plots of land. Typical subsistence crops are corn, beans, rice, tomatoes, onions, peppers, bananas, oranges, and avocados. Cash-crop farmers produce crops for sale, usually concentrating on a single commodity. Small cash-croppers sell their produce to dealers; the dealers and the large farmers sell to international markets. *Fincas*, large estates owned by investors and worked by sharecroppers (laborers who work the fields for a share of the profits and a place to live), produce most of El Salvador's cash crops.

Although some farmers produce food for their families, most crops are grown on large estates and sold.

Since the middle of the 19th century, coffee has been the outstanding cash crop, having replaced cocoa and indigo as El Salvador's most important export. With an annual production of 132,400 tons (146,000 metric tons), tiny El Salvador is the world's third largest producer of coffee, after Brazil and Colombia. Coffee accounts for about 45 percent of the country's earnings from exports.

Coffee bushes grow well in the rich soils and temperate climates of the volcanic highlands. Laborers hand-pick the bright red berries between October and February; women and children often earn a little money by working as pickers. At the processing plants, called *beneficios*, the berries dry in the sun. When they have dried into hard, dark brown beans, workers pack them into bags made of locally grown henequen fibers and ship them to the ports for export.

During the 1950s, cotton gained importance as a cash crop. Growers discovered that it flourished in the hot, damp lowlands—as long as it was protected by chemical insecticides. Today, cotton and clothing together account for approximately 15 percent of the country's total export income. However, the Salvadorans are paying a high price for becoming successful cotton growers. They have used insecticides so extensively that much of the soil in the cotton-growing areas has been damaged. Even worse, El Salvador's rate of insecticide poisoning among farm workers is the highest in Central America.

Some agricultural products grow only in small amounts and limited areas. For example, the Apaneca region, near Ahuachapan, is called El Salvador's flower garden. Markets throughout the country sell lilies, roses, carnations, orchids, and other flowers from Apaneca. Sesame seed is produced near La Unión. The lowlands between Sonsonate and Acajutla yield more than half the nation's annual production of balsam.

Industry and manufacturing boomed in El Salvador in the 1950s. Many foreign governments and companies built factories there because the Salvadorans would work for very low wages. Gradually, wages and living conditions for industrial workers began to improve. During the

1960s, the country's manufacturing output increased by about 8 percent each year. This was the highest rate of industrial growth in Latin America.

But the political strife of the 1970s and 1980s slowed or reversed this rate of growth. Many foreign companies stopped investing in Salvadoran businesses because they feared a complete breakdown of order in the country. In addition, many wealthy Salvadorans chose

Farm workers spray frijoles plants with insecticide. The use of such chemicals has caused serious health problems.

to send their money out of the country for safekeeping, rather than to invest it in development projects at home. Warfare and sabotage also caused direct damage to factories and the ports and railways that served them. From 1979 to 1990, overall losses from damage and from reduced exports were estimated at $2.2 billion—a devastating figure for El Salvador's small economy.

Since the end of the civil war in the early 1990s, manufacturing has grown to account for about 19 percent of the country's annual production. The chief products are beverages, food, petroleum products, chemicals, textiles, and apparel.

Foreign trade is an important part of El Salvador's economy. The country's primary exports are coffee, cotton, and sugarcane. Leading imports include foodstuffs, chemical products, crude petroleum, and cement. El Salvador trades primarily with the United States, Germany, Japan, Mexico, and Venezuela. In 1995, El Salvador joined in the formation of the Association of Caribbean States (ACS), a group of 12 nations seeking to promote free trade in the region.

When tourism became a profitable industry in the Caribbean islands in the 1950s, Salvadorans hoped that their country's unusual black beaches and striking volcanic scenery would lure travelers and tourists. To attract tourists, however, Salvadoran developers needed to invest in expensive resorts and hotels. Just when many such development projects were nearing completion, guerrilla warfare broke out. With the return of peace, the tourist trade began to grow in the 1990s. A big source of tourists was the nearly 1 million Salvadorans living in the United States who began traveling back regularly to visit their homeland.

A crucial fact about the Salvadoran economy is that about 1 percent of the landowners continue to control more than 40 percent of the agricultural land. This small number of people receive a very large percentage of the national income. At the other end of the economic scale, hundreds of thousands of poor Salvadorans—many of them landless and jobless—live on the equivalent of a few U.S. dollars per month. About 40 percent of the population lives below the poverty level. The official unemployment rate fell below 10 percent by the mid-1990s, but many people estimated the real figure to be much higher.

Transportation

El Salvador's network of roads covers 7,600 miles (12,250 kilometers), but only 1,080 miles (1,740 kilometers) are paved. The international Pan-American Highway runs through El Salvador's central region, from Guatemala to Honduras; the Inter-American Highway follows a parallel course along the coast. A network of secondary roads connect these two main highways and serves all parts of the country except a few remote northern regions.

There are only about 96,000 passenger cars in El Salvador. Most of them belong to wealthy people or to the government; they are scarce outside of the cities. The poorer folk travel by train, truck, or bus.

Railways, operated by a government branch, connect the major cities and the seaports along 375 miles (600 kilometers) of track. They are used more for cargo hauling than for passenger travel. One important railway line runs to the Guatemalan city of Puerto Barrios, giving El Salvador access to a Caribbean port. Ilopango Field, 5 miles (8 km) from San Salvador, is El Salvador's international airport. Santa Ana and San Miguel have smaller airports for domestic flights.

Infants and children are cared for by nurses dispatched by UNICEF. International aid programs supplement the country's own services.

Government and Public Services

El Salvador is divided into 14 departments, each with a capital city. Each department has a number of *distritos* (districts), which in turn are divided into *municipios* (townships). The president appoints the governor of each department, and the voters elect the mayor and council of each municipio. All Salvadorans age 18 and older may vote, although the turnout at elections is sometimes poor.

The president and the 84 members of the Legislative Assembly are also elected by popular vote. The assembly makes the nation's laws and can appoint the president and the vice president if the popular vote is evenly divided. It also selects the ten judges of the Supreme Court of Justice, which interprets the law. Municipal and departmental courts handle criminal and civil cases.

El Salvador's army has been very important in the country's political affairs since 1932. One of the demands of the rebel forces during the civil war was that the army dismiss the powerful and very conservative military commanders. The 1992 peace treaty did promise a reform of the military, and the size of the armed forces declined in the 1990s. By 1996 the army had been reduced to 28,400 members, the air force to 1,600 members, and the navy to 1,100 members. (At the height of the civil war, by comparison, the country had 63,000 men in the armed forces.) All Salvadoran men between the ages of 18 and 30 are required to give at least one year of military service.

In addition to the regular military, several public security forces existed in El Salvador until the early 1990s. These organizations worked with the army to control political activities throughout the country, and they were often accused of involvement in murder and torture. Under the terms of the 1992 peace treaty, these discredited units were disbanded, and a new civilian police force was created to replace them.

Health Care

Many parts of El Salvador have poor health care and sanitation facilities. Diseases caused by poor sanitation, such as typhoid fever, amoebic dysentery, and bacillic dysentery, are common in rural areas. In addition, much of the country harbors the *anopheles* mosquito, which carries the tropical

Primitive conditions in rural areas increase problems of sanitation and health.

disease malaria. Heart disease, tuberculosis, and respiratory diseases such as bronchitis and emphysema also kill many Salvadorans each year. The leading causes of death, however, are homicide and violent injury. Life expectancy is 65.4 years for men and 72.5 years for women.

El Salvador has only one doctor for every 2,000 people, and the doctors are concentrated in the cities. Hospitals, also limited to cities and large towns, have one bed for every 922 people. Many Indians and rural ladinos—especially in areas where there is no modern medical care—believe in folk medicine or witchcraft. Their beliefs include the *mal de ojo* ("evil eye" or curse), the *susto* (loss of the soul through fright), and the *hijillo* (sickness caused by an evil spirit from a corpse). Peasants seek the help of *curanderos* (witch doctors), who use herbal medicines, massage, and prayers, as well as modern drugs when they are available, to treat illnesses.

Education

The Ministry of Education runs all of El Salvador's public and private schools. Education is free, and all students are required by law to attend five years of primary school. But due to the severe shortage of schools and teachers, especially in rural areas, many children never attend school. About 40 percent of those who begin primary school do not finish, either because they are needed to help their parents on the family farm or because the compulsory education law is not enforced. About 71.5 percent of the adult population is categorized as literate; many of these people, however, can read or write only their names and a few simple words and phrases.

El Salvador has about 4,000 primary schools, with 26,000 teachers and over 1 million students. It has 240 secondary schools, with 5,000 teachers for 118,000 students. Nearly 78,000 students are attending college and other institutions of higher learning. The University of El Salvador, Delgado University, and the Central American University are the most prominent.

The government promotes universal schooling, from rural one-room schoolhouses to modern universities.

One aspect of Salvadoran education deserves special attention. Although teachers are in short supply, El Salvador has pioneered among Latin American countries the use of television in education. Government-sponsored programs have installed televisions in many country schools. Videotaped or closed-circuit lessons have brought education to some poor rural areas for the first time. Televised reading lessons for adults have begun in some locations. Perhaps television will help the Salvadoran government reach its goal of giving every citizen a basic education.

The Cerron Grande hydroelectric project, built in 1972 with more than $38 million in Inter-American Development Bank funds, was bombed in 1984.

Today and Tomorrow

Life in El Salvador was disrupted by civil war for over 12 years. In a country already poor and struggling, the battles between the government and the leftist guerrillas caused enormous damage to El Salvador's economy. In 1984, for example, guerrillas seized the Cerron Grande Dam and hydroelectric plant. In ten hours of fighting, 120 men were killed and property worth $3.5 million was destroyed.

Overall, approximately 75,000 Salvadorans were killed in the civil war. Most of these casualties were civilians. According to the 1993 report of a commission sponsored by the United Nations, the government forces were responsible for most of the deaths. Some of the atrocities shocked the world. In November 1983, an army battalion that had been trained in the United States massacred a village of more than 100 men, women, and children. The massacre occurred because the soldiers believed that the villagers were sheltering guerrilla fighters.

Some of El Salvador's guerrillas were linked to Communist powers. Under President Ronald Reagan, the United States supported the government forces because it felt that a guerrilla victory would result in the country's becoming a Communist nation. Many guerrilla forces and other observers disputed this view, however, arguing that the rebel forces were fighting to establish political and economic freedoms long denied to the majority of El Salvador's population.

Because of the war, a steady stream of Salvadorans left the country. Many came to the United States. A dispute arose in the United States over whether the Salvadorans were political refugees who ought to be granted asylum or illegal immigrants who ought to be expelled. Over 250 U.S. churches formed the Sanctuary movement to assist Salvadoran (and Guatemalan) refugees in finding residences and jobs. The U.S. government strongly opposed these efforts.

The farmers and the federal government still struggle to find an equitable solution for the problems of land distribution and agrarian debt.

Since the peace treaty was signed ending the civil war, many changes have taken place in El Salvador. The government has greatly reduced the size of the armed forces. A new civilian national police has been organized to replace the old internal security forces that had been accused of violating human rights. Many former guerrillas have been integrated into the political life of the country, and the guerrilla armies have been reorganized into political parties. The process of transferring some land from wealthy owners to poor farmers has begun, although at a slow pace.

Much anger and political disagreement are still evident in the country's politics. The government has been torn by differences over such issues as protection of the rights of workers and expenditures on education and health. In 1994, and again in 1995, former soldiers occupied the National Assembly, holding hostages and demanding benefits that had been promised to them in the 1992 peace treaty. The crisis was ended peacefully in both cases, but further outbreaks of hostility remained possible.

In 1996 prisoners throughout the country staged hunger strikes demanding better conditions. Most of them were awaiting trial, and one of their demands was for speedier trials. President Calderón Sol ultimately agreed to some of the inmates' demands, and he promised to construct more prisons to reduce overcrowding.

Despite the promising developments since 1992, many social problems continue to plague El Salvador. The bloodshed and agony of the 1980s have ended, but the achievement of a lasting peace remains a long-term goal for Salvadorans.

◄ G L O S S A R Y ►

Audencia   A captaincy general, or region of a colony governed by a captain general (an administrator of combined military and civilian rank, usually appointed by the Spanish crown).

Cabilda   A council of white men set up to govern a native Indian community in a Spanish colony.

Chirimia   A flute used in native Salvadoran music.

Compadrazgo   The close, lifelong relationship between a child's father and its godfather. The father and the godfather, or *compadres*, are regarded as something like blood brothers.

Conquistadores   The mercenary soldiers and adventurers who claimed much of Mexico, Central America, and South America for Spain in the 16th century. Some of them amassed huge fortunes, but many more died from disease or Indian attack. They became notorious for their cruel treatment of the native Indian peoples.

Creole   A white Spanish-American born in the New World colonies.

Curandero   A witch doctor. Rural Indians and ladinos consult curanderos for herbal remedies, prayers, and protection against curses or evil spirits.

Finca   A large agricultural estate owned by investors and worked by hired laborers or sharecroppers.

Henequén   Also called sisal. A plant whose tough fibers can be woven into cloth, rope, mats, and other goods.

Intendencia	A governorship, or region administered by a colonial governor (an *intendiente*).
Jeu jeu	A rural dance based on a Mayan rain dance. In the Izalco region of El Salvador, jeu jeu dancers act out mock battles between the Spanish and the Indians.
Jiquilite	The plant that produces the deep-blue dye indigo.
Junta	A council of military officers; usually used to describe officers who forcibly seize control of a government or state.
Ladino	Anyone who wears Western-style clothing and follows Spanish-American customs. All whites and mestizos are ladinos; Indians who have abandoned traditional native ways are also ladinos.
Marimba	A piano-like instrument that has hollow gourds instead of keys. The gourds are struck with padded sticks to produce a chiming sound.
Mestizo	Someone of mixed European and Indian ancestry.
Papusa	A cornmeal cake stuffed with chopped meat and spices, usually sold at outdoor stalls.
Reducción	The Spanish policy of moving Indians from their scattered villages into mission settlements. Reducción was supposed to make it easier to convert the Indians to Christianity, but it also made it easier to prevent them from rebelling.
Repartimiento	A system of land distribution that gave huge tracts in the New World to wealthy or powerful Spaniards. The Indians who lived on the land were forced to become laborers for the new landowners.

◄INDEX►

PICTURE CREDITS

Bettmann Archive (p. 27); Inter-American Development Bank (pp. 20, 72, 82, 84–85, 92, 94); Ellen S. Knudsen (pp. 24, 25, 49, 50 above); Library of Congress (pp. 28, 32, 35, 37, 38, 42); David Mangurian (pp. 74–75); Organization of American States (pp. 18–19, 22, 58, 90, 96); Peace Corps (pp. 14, 18, 51 above, 52 above, 53 below, 54–55 below, 56 above, 62, 69, 80); Carl Purcell (pp. 51 below, 52 below, 53 above, 63, 67); Unicef (p. 88); United Nations (pp. 2, 56 below, 64–65); UPI Bettmann Newsphotos (pp. 40, 45, 47, 77); U.S. Department of Housing and Urban Development (p. 16); World Bank (pp. 50 below, 52, 55 above, 66).